QUICK COOKING

Fast Fixin' Recipes with
VELVEETA® Process Cheese Spread

Publications International, Ltd.

Favorite All Time Recipes is published by Publications International, Ltd., 7373 N. Cicero Ave., Lincolnwood, IL 60646.

Pictured on the front cover: Cheesy Chicken Vesuvio (*page 29*).

Pictured on the back cover: VELVEETA® Process Cheese Spread Salsa Dip (*page 12*).

ISBN: 0-7853-1085-1

Manufactured in U.S.A.

8   7   6   5   4   3   2   1

PREPARATION/COOKING TIMES: Each of these recipes was developed and tested by food professionals in The Kraft Creative Kitchens. The preparation times are based on the amount of time required to assemble the recipe before baking, cooking, chilling, freezing or serving. These times include preparation steps such as chopping, mixing, cooking rice, pasta, vegetables, etc.

MICROWAVE COOKING: Microwave ovens vary in wattage. The microwave cooking times given in this publication are approximate. Use the cooking times as guidelines and check for doneness before adding more time. Consult manufacturer's instructions for suitable microwave-safe dishes.

CONTENTS

APPETIZER FAVORITES

PESTO AND APPLE TART

(photographed on previous page)

¾ cup parsley sprigs
½ cup walnut pieces
3 tablespoons olive oil
2 tablespoons lemon juice
2 teaspoons dried basil leaves

2 medium apples, cored, thinly sliced
½ (15 oz.) pkg. refrigerated pie crust (1 crust)
¾ lb. VELVEETA Pasteurized Process Cheese Spread, sliced

Preheat oven to 450°.

Place parsley, walnuts, oil, 1 tablespoon lemon juice and basil in food processor container with steel blade attached; process until walnuts are finely chopped.

Toss apples with remaining lemon juice.

Unfold pie crust. Place in 10-inch tart pan. Prick several times with fork.

Bake 8 minutes; remove from oven. Reduce oven temperature to 400°.

Spread parsley mixture over crust. Arrange apples and process cheese spread over parsley mixture.

Bake 10 minutes or until crust is lightly browned. Sprinkle with additional chopped parsley and fresh basil leaves, if desired.   *10 servings*

Prep time: 20 minutes
Cooking time: 10 minutes

Variation: Omit tart pan. Unfold pie crust onto greased cookie sheet; prick with fork. Continue as directed.

APPETIZER BITES

1 (6 oz.) pkg. OSCAR MAYER Smoked Cooked Ham Slices, chopped
¼ lb. VELVEETA Pasteurized Process Cheese Spread, cubed
½ cup KRAFT Real Mayonnaise

1 tablespoon Dijon mustard
1 tablespoon chopped parsley
9 frozen phyllo sheets (18 × 14 inch), thawed
¼ cup PARKAY Margarine, melted

Preheat oven to 350°.

Mix together all ingredients except phyllo and margarine. Fold each phyllo sheet into quarters; cut crosswise in half to form two 7 × 4½-inch rectangles. Do not unfold. Repeat with remaining phyllo sheets.

Spoon 1 tablespoon ham mixture onto one end of each rectangle. Fold short sides of rectangle over filling; roll lengthwise to form appetizer bundle. Place, seam side down, on foil-covered cookie sheet. Brush with margarine.

Bake 15 minutes or until lightly browned.   *1½ dozen*

Prep time: 15 minutes
Cooking time: 15 minutes

HOT BROCCOLI DIP

1 (1½ lb.) round sourdough bread
    loaf
½ cup chopped celery
½ cup chopped red pepper
¼ cup chopped onion
2 tablespoons PARKAY Margarine

1 lb. VELVEETA Pasteurized Process
    Cheese Spread, cubed
1 (10 oz.) pkg. frozen chopped
    broccoli, thawed, drained
¼ teaspoon dried rosemary leaves,
    crushed
Few drops hot pepper sauce

Preheat oven to 350°.

Cut lengthwise slice from top of bread loaf; remove center, leaving 1-inch-thick shell. Cut removed bread into bite-size pieces. Cover shell with top of bread; place on cookie sheet with bread pieces.

Bake 15 minutes. Cool slightly.

Saute celery, peppers and onions in margarine. Reduce heat to low. Add process cheese spread; stir until melted. Stir in broccoli, rosemary and hot pepper sauce; heat thoroughly, stirring constantly.

Spoon into bread loaf; serve hot with toasted bread pieces and vegetable dippers.
6 to 8 servings

Prep time: 25 minutes

MICROWAVE: • Prepare bread shell as directed. • Microwave celery, peppers, onions and margarine in 2-quart bowl on HIGH 1 minute. • Stir in process cheese spread, broccoli, rosemary and hot pepper sauce. Microwave 5 to 6 minutes or until hot, stirring after 3 minutes. • Spoon into bread loaf. Serve hot with toasted bread pieces and vegetable dippers.

Microwave cooking time: 7 minutes

Variation: Omit bread loaf. Prepare dip as directed. Serve in bowl with vegetable dippers.

Mexican Sausage Pie

MEXICAN SAUSAGE PIE

½ lb. chorizo sausage
1 (1 lb.) loaf frozen whole-wheat bread dough, thawed
1 (10 oz.) pkg. frozen chopped broccoli, thawed, well drained
1 cup whole kernel corn, well drained

½ lb. VELVEETA Mexican Pasteurized Process Cheese Spread with Jalapeño Pepper, sliced
1 egg yolk
1 teaspoon cold water
1 tablespoon cornmeal

Preheat oven to 375°.

Remove sausage from casing. Brown sausage; drain. Cool.

Roll two-thirds of dough to 11-inch circle on lightly floured surface. Press onto bottom and up sides of greased 9-inch springform pan.

Layer broccoli, corn, sausage and process cheese spread over dough in pan.

Roll remaining dough to 10-inch circle; cut into eight wedges. Place over filling, overlapping edges and sealing ends to bottom crust. Brush with combined egg yolk and water. Sprinkle with cornmeal.

Bake 35 to 40 minutes or until deep golden brown. Let stand 10 minutes. Garnish as desired.
10 servings

Prep time: 20 minutes
Cooking time: 40 minutes

Microwave Tip: • To cook sausage, remove sausage from casing. Crumble into 1-quart bowl. • Microwave on HIGH 4 to 6 minutes or until sausage is cooked, stirring after 3 minutes; drain.

CHEESY GUACAMOLE

¼ lb. VELVEETA Pasteurized Process Cheese Spread, cubed
½ cup sour cream
2 avocados, peeled, coarsely chopped
1 tomato, coarsely chopped

½ small onion, coarsely chopped
1 fresh jalapeño pepper, seeded, coarsely chopped
1 tablespoon lemon juice
Few drops hot pepper sauce

Place all ingredients in food processor container with steel blade attached; process until blended. Serve with tortilla chips.
3 cups

Prep time: 10 minutes

VELVEETA® SALSA DIP
Process Cheese Spread

1 lb. VELVEETA Pasteurized Process
    Cheese Spread, cubed
1 (8 oz.) jar salsa

2 tablespoons chopped cilantro
    (optional)

Stir together process cheese spread and salsa over low heat until process cheese spread is melted. Stir in cilantro.

Serve hot with tortilla chips or broiled green, red or yellow pepper wedges. Garnish with green pepper cut into decorative shape.

3 cups

Prep time: 10 minutes

MICROWAVE: • Microwave process cheese spread and salsa in 1½-quart bowl on HIGH 5 minutes or until process cheese spread is melted, stirring after 3 minutes. Stir in cilantro. • Serve as directed.

Microwave cooking time: 5 minutes

Variation: Substitute 14½-oz. can tomatoes, drained, chopped, for salsa.

CHEESY FOCACCIA

3 cups buttermilk baking mix
2 cups (8 ozs.) VELVEETA Shredded
    Pasteurized Process Cheese
    Food
1 teaspoon dried basil leaves,
    crushed

¼ teaspoon dried oregano leaves,
    crushed
1 cup milk
6 tablespoons olive oil

Preheat oven to 375°.

Stir together baking mix, process cheese food and seasonings. Add milk; mix well.

Coat bottom of 15 x 10 x 1-inch jelly roll pan with 2 tablespoons olive oil. Pat dough evenly into pan with floured hands. Make indentations with fingertips at 1-inch intervals over entire surface of dough. Brush remaining olive oil evenly over dough.

Bake 20 minutes or until golden brown. Cut into rectangles; serve warm.

Approximately 3 dozen

Prep time: 10 minutes
Cooking time: 20 minutes

VELVEETA® Salsa Dip

Crispy Oriental Wontons

CRISPY ORIENTAL WONTONS

½ lb. ground pork
1 cup (4 ozs.) VELVEETA Shredded
    Pasteurized Process Cheese
    Food
2 tablespoons green onion slices

1 teaspoon minced peeled ginger
    root
1 teaspoon sesame oil (optional)
32 wonton wrappers
    Sesame seeds
    Dipping Sauce

Preheat oven to 425°.

Brown meat; drain. Mix together meat, process cheese food, onions, ginger root and sesame oil.

For each wonton, place scant tablespoonful meat mixture in center of one wonton wrapper. Bring corners together over meat mixture; twist and pinch together, enclosing meat mixture in dough. Flatten bottom slightly. Place on cookie sheet. Brush lightly with water; sprinkle with sesame seeds.

Bake 10 to 12 minutes or until golden brown. Serve warm with Dipping Sauce.

32 appetizers

DIPPING SAUCE

2 tablespoons soy sauce
1 tablespoon cold water

1 tablespoon rice wine
    (optional)

Mix together ingredients until blended.

¼ cup

Prep time: 25 minutes
Cooking time: 12 minutes

HOLIDAY VEGETABLE NIBBLES

½ lb. VELVEETA Pasteurized Process
    Cheese Spread, cubed
¼ cup sour cream
¼ cup finely chopped green or red
    pepper

1 tablespoon chopped green onion
½ teaspoon dried tarragon leaves,
    crushed

Beat all ingredients at medium speed with electric mixer until well blended. Pipe or spread onto assorted vegetable dippers or serve with crackers. *1 cup*

Prep time: 10 minutes

Suggested vegetable dippers: Pea pods, cherry tomatoes, cucumber slices, jicama slices, carrot sticks, celery sticks or Belgian endive.

WEEKDAY DINNERS

WHITE FISH WITH RED PEPPER SAUCE

(photographed on previous page)

1 lb. fine-textured fish fillets (such
    as flounder, sole or whitefish)
2 tablespoons PARKAY Margarine
1 tablespoon dried oregano leaves,
    crushed

1 (7 oz.) jar roasted red peppers,
    undrained
¼ lb. VELVEETA Pasteurized Process
    Cheese Spread, cubed

Fry fish on both sides in margarine and oregano over medium-high heat until fish flakes easily with fork. Remove fish from skillet; keep warm.

Place red peppers in blender or food processor container with steel blade attached. Cover; process until smooth. Pour into skillet. Reduce heat to low.

Add process cheese spread to peppers in skillet; stir until process cheese spread is melted. Serve over fish. Garnish with fresh oregano. *4 servings*

Prep time: 15 minutes

MICROWAVE: • Reduce margarine to 1 tablespoon. • Arrange fish in 12 × 8-inch baking dish with thickest portions toward outside of dish. • Microwave margarine and oregano in small bowl on HIGH 30 seconds or until margarine is melted; pour over fish. Cover with plastic wrap; vent. • Microwave fish 5 minutes, turning dish after 3 minutes. Let stand, covered, 2 to 3 minutes or until fish flakes easily with fork. • Puree red peppers as directed. Pour into 1-quart bowl. Add process cheese spread. • Microwave 2 to 4 minutes or until process cheese spread is melted, stirring after 1½ minutes. • Serve over fish. Garnish with fresh oregano.

Microwave cooking time: 10 minutes plus standing

SAVORY BACON 'N CHEESE PASTA

1 (12 oz.) pkg. VELVEETA Shells &
    Cheese Dinner
8 OSCAR MAYER Bacon Slices,
    crisply cooked, crumbled

1 (9 oz.) pkg. frozen cut green
    beans, thawed, drained
2 tablespoons chopped fresh
    chives

Prepare Dinner as directed on package.

Stir in remaining ingredients; continue cooking until thoroughly heated.

4 to 6 servings

Prep time: 20 minutes

▨▪ MICROWAVE: • Prepare Dinner as directed on package. • Stir in remaining ingredients. • Microwave 3 to 5 minutes or until thoroughly heated, stirring every 2 minutes.

Microwave cooking time: 20 minutes

TURKEY ENCHILADAS CON QUESO

1 (8 oz.) pkg. PHILADELPHIA BRAND
    Cream Cheese, softened
¼ cup green onion slices
1 cup chopped LOUIS RICH Oven
    Roasted Boneless Turkey Breast
8 (6 inch) corn tortillas

Oil
¾ lb. VELVEETA Mexican Pasteurized
    Process Cheese Spread with
    Jalapeño Pepper, cubed
1 cup chopped tomato
¼ cup milk

Preheat oven to 350°.

Mix together cream cheese and onions until well blended. Stir in turkey.

Brush tortillas lightly with oil. Stack flour tortillas on plate. Microwave on HIGH 30 seconds or until softened. Repeat with remaining tortillas.

Spoon ¼ cup turkey mixture onto each tortilla; roll up. Place, seam side down, in 12 × 8-inch baking dish.

Stir together process cheese spread, ½ cup tomatoes and milk in saucepan over low heat until process cheese spread is melted.

Pour sauce over enchiladas. Top with remaining tomatoes; cover with foil.

Bake 25 to 30 minutes or until thoroughly heated.   *4 servings*

Prep time: 15 minutes
Cooking time: 30 minutes

▨▪ MICROWAVE: • Assemble enchiladas as directed. • Microwave process cheese spread, ½ cup tomatoes and milk in 1-quart bowl on HIGH 2 to 4 minutes or until process cheese spread is melted, stirring every minute. • Pour sauce over enchiladas; top with remaining tomatoes. • Microwave 12 to 14 minutes or until thoroughly heated, turning dish after 6 minutes.

Microwave cooking time: 18 minutes

TORTELLINI PRIMAVERA

2 medium carrots, diagonally
  sliced, halved
1 medium zucchini, thinly sliced
1 cup mushroom slices
1 medium red pepper, coarsely
  chopped
2 tablespoons PARKAY Margarine

½ lb. VELVEETA Pasteurized Process
  Cheese Spread, cubed
¼ cup milk
1 teaspoon Italian seasoning
8 to 9 ozs. fresh or frozen, meat- or
  cheese-filled tortellini, cooked,
  drained

Saute vegetables in margarine in large skillet 5 to 7 minutes or until carrots are crisp-tender. Reduce heat to low.

Add process cheese spread, milk and seasoning; stir until process cheese spread is melted.

Stir in tortellini; continue cooking until thoroughly heated.   *4 servings*

Prep time: 25 minutes

MICROWAVE: • Decrease milk to 1 tablespoon. • Microwave carrots, peppers and margarine in 2-quart casserole on HIGH 4 to 5 minutes or until vegetables are crisp-tender, stirring after 2 minutes. • Add zucchini and mushrooms. Microwave 2 to 3 minutes or until zucchini is tender; drain. • Stir in process cheese spread, milk and seasoning. • Microwave 2 to 3 minutes or until process cheese spread is melted, stirring after each minute. • Stir in tortellini. • Microwave 1 to 2 minutes or until thoroughly heated.

Microwave cooking time: 13 minutes

EASY CHICKEN IN CURRANT WINE SAUCE

4 boneless skinless chicken breasts
  (approx. 1¼ lbs.)
2 tablespoons PARKAY Margarine
¼ cup KRAFT Red Currant Jelly
1 tablespoon dry white wine or cold
  water

½ cup seedless grapes
½ cup (2 ozs.) VELVEETA Shredded
  Pasteurized Process Cheese
  Food

Cook chicken in margarine over medium heat 3 to 5 minutes on each side or until tender; remove to warm platter. Stir jelly and wine into drippings in skillet; simmer 5 minutes. Return chicken to skillet; turn to coat with glaze. Stir in grapes. Top chicken with process cheese food; cover. Heat until process cheese food is melted.

4 servings

Prep time: 20 minutes

Tortellini Primavera

SZECHWAN PORK CHOPS

4 pork loin chops, ½ to ¾ inch thick
1 garlic clove, minced
2 tablespoons peanut oil
2 tablespoons dry sherry (optional)
½ teaspoon ground ginger
¼ teaspoon crushed red pepper
¼ teaspoon sesame seed oil (optional)

Milk
¼ lb. VELVEETA Pasteurized Process Cheese Spread, cubed
2 tablespoons chopped unsalted peanuts
1 tablespoon chopped cilantro

Brown chops and garlic in peanut oil in large skillet; pour off all but 1 tablespoon drippings. Reduce heat to medium-low.

Add sherry, ginger, red pepper and sesame seed oil; cover.

Simmer 20 to 25 minutes or until chops are tender. Remove chops to warm platter, reserving pan drippings.

Measure pan drippings. Add enough milk to pan drippings, if necessary, to measure ⅓ cup. Return to skillet. Add process cheese spread; stir until melted.

Spoon sauce over chops; sprinkle with peanuts and cilantro. Serve with hot cooked rice and garnish with red pepper strips. *4 servings*

Prep time: 15 minutes
Cooking time: 25 minutes

Variation: Substitute 1 teaspoon toasted sesame seeds for 2 tablespoons peanuts.

PASTA WITH CHEESY ARTICHOKE SAUCE

½ lb. VELVEETA Pasteurized Process Cheese Spread, cubed
1 (7 oz.) jar roasted red peppers, drained, cut into strips
1 (6½ oz.) jar marinated artichoke hearts, drained, quartered

¼ cup pitted ripe olive halves
1 tablespoon chopped fresh basil
2 teaspoons red wine (optional)
1 garlic clove, minced
8 ozs. fettuccine, cooked, drained

Stir together all ingredients except fettuccine in saucepan over low heat until process cheese spread is melted. Serve over hot fettuccine. *4 servings*

Prep time: 20 minutes

Szechwan Pork Chop

Chicken Fajita Pizzas

CHICKEN FAJITA PIZZAS

4 (6 inch) flour tortillas
1½ cups (6 ozs.) VELVEETA Mexican
    Shredded Pasteurized Process
    Cheese Food
1 cup shredded cooked chicken

½ cup salsa
½ cup chopped green pepper
½ cup chopped seeded tomato
¼ cup pitted ripe olive slices

Preheat oven to 350°.

Place tortillas on cookie sheet; sprinkle 2 tablespoons process cheese food over each tortilla.

Bake 4 to 5 minutes or until process cheese food is melted.

Toss chicken with salsa; spoon over tortillas.

Toss remaining process cheese food with peppers; sprinkle over chicken mixture.

Bake 7 to 10 minutes or until thoroughly heated and process cheese food is melted. Top with remaining ingredients.
4 servings

Prep time: 20 minutes
Cooking time: 10 minutes

EASY CHICKEN NOODLE SKILLET DINNER

1 garlic clove, minced
2 tablespoons PARKAY Margarine
2 cups quartered mushrooms
¼ cup dry sherry or chicken broth
4 boneless skinless chicken breasts
    (approx. 1¼ lbs.), cut into
    1-inch pieces

¾ lb. VELVEETA Pasteurized Process
    Cheese Spread, cubed
1 (10 oz.) pkg. frozen peas, thawed,
    drained
¼ teaspoon pepper
4 cups (8 ozs.) wide noodles,
    cooked, drained

Saute garlic in margarine in large skillet. Add mushrooms and 2 tablespoons sherry. Cook 3 minutes, stirring occasionally.

Add chicken; cook 5 to 7 minutes or until chicken is no longer pink. Reduce heat to low.

Stir in remaining sherry, process cheese spread, peas and pepper. Cook 8 to 10 minutes or until process cheese spread is melted, stirring occasionally.

Stir in noodles; heat thoroughly.
6 servings

Prep time: 30 minutes

Corn Bread Chili Pot Pie

CORN BREAD CHILI POT PIE

½ lb. ground beef
2 cups Black and White Bean Chili
(see page 32 for recipe)

1 cup (4 ozs.) VELVEETA Mexican
Shredded Pasteurized Process
Cheese Food
1 (11.5 oz.) pkg. refrigerated corn
bread twists

Preheat oven to 375°.

Brown meat; drain. Add chili; heat thoroughly, stirring occasionally. Stir in process cheese food; spoon into 9-inch pie plate.

Unroll dough; separate into strips. Join together short ends of each of two strips to form one 8-inch strip. (You should have eight 8-inch strips.) Arrange in lattice design over chili.

Bake 15 to 17 minutes or until corn bread is golden brown.   *6 servings*

Prep time: 20 minutes
Cooking time: 17 minutes

RISOTTO WITH SAUSAGE

½ lb. Italian sausage
½ cup chopped onion
1⅔ cups cold water
½ teaspoon dried oregano leaves,
crushed

1⅔ cups MINUTE Premium Long-Grain
Rice, uncooked
2 tablespoons chopped parsley
1 cup (4 ozs.) VELVEETA Shredded
Pasteurized Process Cheese
Food

Remove sausage from casing. Brown sausage; drain. Add onions; cook until tender.

Stir in water and oregano; bring to full boil. Stir in rice and parsley. Cover; remove from heat. Let stand 5 minutes; fluff with fork.

Add process cheese food; stir until melted.   *6 servings*

Prep time: 15 minutes

MIDWEST MEAT LOAF WITH CHEESY BEER SAUCE

½ lb. VELVEETA Pasteurized Process
   Cheese Spread, cubed
¼ cup beer or milk
2 teaspoons dry mustard
1 lb. ground beef

⅓ cup old fashioned or quick oats,
   uncooked
¼ cup catsup
¼ cup chopped onion

Preheat oven to 350°.

Stir together process cheese spread, beer and mustard in saucepan over low heat until process cheese spread is melted.

Reserve ¾ cup process cheese spread sauce. Mix remaining ¼ cup process cheese spread sauce with meat, oats, catsup and onions until well blended.

Place in 10 x 6-inch baking dish. Shape into 8 x 3-inch loaf.

Bake 40 minutes. Serve with reserved process cheese spread sauce, heated.

4 servings

Prep time: 15 minutes
Cooking time: 40 minutes

MICROWAVE: • Microwave process cheese spread, beer and mustard in 1½-quart bowl on HIGH 3 to 5 minutes or until process cheese spread is melted, stirring every 2 minutes. • Prepare meat loaf as directed except for baking; cover with wax paper. • Microwave 10 to 14 minutes or to desired doneness, rotating dish after 6 minutes. Let stand 10 minutes before serving. • Microwave reserved process cheese spread sauce 1 minute or until thoroughly heated. Serve with meat loaf.

Microwave cooking time: 20 minutes plus standing

BAKED CHIMICHANGAS WITH SALSA

1 lb. ground beef
1 (1.25 oz.) pkg. taco seasoning
   mix
½ cup cold water
2 cups (8 ozs.) VELVEETA Shredded
   Pasteurized Process Cheese
   Food

1 (8 oz.) pkg. refrigerated crescent
   dinner rolls
¾ cup chopped tomato
¼ cup chopped onion
1 tablespoon chopped cilantro

Preheat oven to 375°.

Brown meat; drain. Add seasoning mix and water; bring to boil. Reduce heat to low; simmer 5 minutes, stirring occasionally.

Add 1¼ cups process cheese food; stir until melted.

Unroll dough to form four rectangles; press perforations together to seal.

Place ⅔ cup meat mixture on each rectangle. Fold dough lengthwise in half over filling; press edges together with fork to seal. Place in 12 × 8-inch baking dish.

Bake 15 minutes or until golden brown. Sprinkle with remaining process cheese food. Top with combined tomatoes, onions and cilantro. Serve with shredded lettuce and sour cream. *4 servings*

Prep time: 20 minutes
Cooking time: 15 minutes

CHEESY CHICKEN VESUVIO

4 boneless skinless chicken breasts (approx. 1¼ lbs.)	**3 tablespoons chopped parsley**
1 garlic clove, minced	**2 teaspoons chopped fresh oregano**
1 tablespoon olive oil	**½ lb. VELVEETA Pasteurized Process Cheese Spread, cubed**
¼ cup dry white wine or chicken broth	

Brown chicken and garlic in oil in large skillet.

Add all remaining ingredients except process cheese spread; cover. Simmer 20 minutes or until chicken is tender.

Remove chicken to serving platter; keep warm. Reduce heat to low.

Add process cheese spread to drippings in skillet; stir until process cheese spread is melted. Serve over chicken. *4 servings*

Prep time: 20 minutes
Cooking time: 20 minutes

MICROWAVE: • Reduce wine to 2 tablespoons. • Microwave garlic and oil in 8-inch square baking dish on HIGH 1 minute. • Add chicken, wine, parsley and oregano. Cover with plastic wrap; vent. • Microwave 7 to 9 minutes or until chicken is tender, turning chicken over and rotating dish after 4 minutes. Remove chicken to serving platter; keep warm. • Add process cheese spread to drippings in dish. • Microwave 2 minutes or until process cheese spread is melted, stirring every minute. Serve over chicken.

Microwave cooking time: 12 minutes

QUICK BEAN CASSOULET

1½ cups diagonally cut carrot slices
3 garlic cloves, minced
2 tablespoons PARKAY Margarine
2 (15½ oz.) cans great Northern white beans, rinsed, drained
¾ lb. smoked sausage slices, halved
1 cup dry white wine or chicken broth

¾ teaspoon rubbed sage
¾ lb. VELVEETA Pasteurized Process Cheese Spread, cubed
1 large tomato, chopped
¼ cup chopped parsley
½ cup fresh bread crumbs

Saute carrots and garlic in 1 tablespoon margarine in Dutch oven 5 to 7 minutes or until carrots are crisp-tender.

Stir in beans, sausage, wine and sage. Bring to boil. Reduce heat to low. Cover; simmer 5 minutes.

Add process cheese spread and tomatoes; stir until process cheese spread is melted. Stir in 3 tablespoons parsley. Spoon into 2-quart casserole or serving bowl.

Melt remaining margarine. Add to combined remaining parsley and bread crumbs; toss lightly. Sprinkle over cassoulet. Garnish with fresh sage.   *Six 1¼-cup servings*

Prep time: 30 minutes

MICROWAVE: • Microwave carrots, garlic and 1 tablespoon margarine in 3-quart casserole on HIGH 3 to 5 minutes or until carrots are crisp-tender. • Add beans, sausage, wine and sage. Microwave 7 to 10 minutes or until thoroughly heated, stirring after 5 minutes. • Stir in process cheese spread and tomatoes. • Microwave 4 to 6 minutes or until process cheese spread is melted, stirring after 3 minutes. Stir in 3 tablespoons parsley. • Prepare crumb topping as directed. Sprinkle over cassoulet. Garnish with fresh sage.

Microwave cooking time: 21 minutes

Quick Bean Cassoulet

MEXICAN MAC 'N CHEESE DINNER

1 (7 oz.) pkg. elbow macaroni
¾ lb. VELVEETA Mexican Pasteurized
    Process Cheese Spread with
    Jalapeño Pepper, cubed
¼ cup milk
1 tablespoon chopped cilantro

1 lb. ground beef
1 (8 oz.) can tomato sauce
½ cup chopped tomato
¼ cup green onion slices
¼ cup pitted ripe olive slices

Cook macaroni according to package directions; drain. Add process cheese spread, milk and cilantro; stir until process cheese spread is melted.

Crumble meat into 1-quart bowl. Microwave on HIGH 5 to 6 minutes or until meat loses pink color when stirred; drain. Stir in tomato sauce.

Spoon half of macaroni mixture into 2-quart casserole; top with meat mixture and remaining macaroni. Cover with lid.

Microwave 5 to 7 minutes or until thoroughly heated, turning dish after 3 minutes. Top with remaining ingredients. *4 to 6 servings*

Prep time: 15 minutes
Microwave cooking time: 13 minutes

CONVENTIONAL: • Preheat oven to 350°. • Prepare macaroni mixture as directed. • Brown meat; drain. Stir in tomato sauce. • Assemble recipe as directed. • Bake, uncovered, 15 minutes or until thoroughly heated. Top with remaining ingredients.

Conventional cooking time: 15 minutes

BLACK AND WHITE BEAN CHILI

½ cup chopped green pepper
½ cup chopped red pepper
½ cup chopped onion
2 tablespoons PARKAY Margarine
1 (15½ oz.) can great Northern
    white beans, rinsed, drained
1 (15 oz.) can black beans, rinsed,
    drained
1 cup cold water

1 (4 oz.) can chopped green
    chilies, undrained
½ teaspoon ground cumin
¼ to ½ teaspoon white or coarse
    grind black pepper
1½ cups (6 ozs.) VELVEETA Mexican
    Shredded Pasteurized Process
    Cheese Food

Saute green and red peppers and onions in margarine. Reduce heat to medium.

Stir in beans, water, chilies, cumin and white pepper. Cook 15 minutes or until thoroughly heated.

Add 1 cup process cheese food; stir until melted.

Top individual servings with remaining process cheese food.   *Six ¾-cup servings*

Prep time: 15 minutes
Cooking time: 15 minutes

MICROWAVE: • Reduce margarine to 1 tablespoon. • Stir together green and red peppers, onions and margarine in 2-quart casserole. Microwave on HIGH 3 to 4 minutes or until vegetables are crisp-tender. • Stir in beans, water, chilies, cumin and white pepper; cover with lid. Microwave 7 to 13 minutes or until thoroughly heated, stirring after 5 minutes. • Add 1 cup process cheese food; stir until melted. • Top individual servings with remaining process cheese food.

Microwave cooking time: 17 minutes

CORNED BEEF & CABBAGE CASSEROLE

2 cups mashed potatoes	1 cup (4 ozs.) VELVEETA Shredded
¼ cup chopped parsley	Pasteurized Process Cheese
2 cups finely chopped cabbage	Food
1½ cups finely chopped cooked	½ cup shredded carrot
corned beef	¼ cup chopped onion
	1 teaspoon caraway seed

Preheat oven to 350°.

Stir together potatoes and parsley; spoon into 2-quart casserole.

Mix together remaining ingredients; spoon over potato mixture.

Bake 35 to 40 minutes or until thoroughly heated.   *6 servings*

Prep time: 20 minutes
Cooking time: 40 minutes

MICROWAVE: • Assemble recipe as directed. • Microwave on HIGH 8 to 12 minutes or until thoroughly heated, turning dish after 5 minutes. Let stand 5 minutes before serving.

Microwave cooking time: 12 minutes plus standing

SPICY CHILAQUILES

¼ lb. chorizo sausage
3 tablespoons oil
8 (6 inch) corn tortillas, cut into
   ½-inch strips
1 cup thin green pepper strips

½ lb. VELVEETA Mexican Pasteurized
   Process Cheese Spread with
   Jalapeño Pepper, cubed
1 medium tomato, chopped

Remove sausage from casing. Brown sausage; drain.

Heat oil in large skillet over medium heat. Add tortilla strips; cook 4 to 5 minutes or until golden brown, stirring constantly.

Add peppers; cook 2 to 3 minutes or until peppers are crisp-tender, stirring constantly. Reduce heat to low.

Add sausage, process cheese spread and tomatoes; stir until process cheese spread begins to melt. Serve with sour cream.   *4 servings*

Prep time: 20 minutes

Variation: Substitute bulk pork sausage for chorizo.

CHEESY HAM CALZONES

1 small onion, chopped
2 tablespoons PARKAY Margarine
2 cups frozen Southern-style hash
   brown potatoes
1½ cups ham cubes

1 cup (4 ozs.) VELVEETA Shredded
   Pasteurized Process Cheese
   Food
1 tablespoon spicy brown mustard
1 (10 oz.) pkg. refrigerated pizza
   crust

Preheat oven to 400°.

Saute onions in margarine. Add potatoes; cook 3 to 5 minutes or until thoroughly heated. Remove from heat. Stir in all remaining ingredients except pizza dough.

Unroll dough; cut into four rectangles. Flatten each rectangle to 7-inch square.

Place ¾ cup ham mixture in center of each square. Fold dough over filling to form triangle; press edges together with fork to seal. Place on greased cookie sheet.

Bake 10 to 12 minutes or until golden brown.   *4 servings*

Prep time: 15 minutes
Cooking time: 12 minutes

Spicy Chilaquiles

Peppery Roast Beef Hash

PEPPERY ROAST BEEF HASH

½ cup chopped red pepper
½ cup green onion slices
¼ cup PARKAY Margarine
4 cups frozen Southern-style hash brown potatoes
2 cups chopped rare cooked roast beef

½ teaspoon salt
¼ to ½ teaspoon black pepper
1 cup (4 ozs.) VELVEETA Shredded Pasteurized Process Cheese Food

Saute red peppers and onions in margarine in 10-inch skillet. Reduce heat to medium-high.

Stir in all remaining ingredients except process cheese food; cover. Cook 10 minutes or until potatoes are cooked and mixture is thoroughly heated.

Stir in process cheese food; cover. Continue cooking 5 minutes or until process cheese food is melted. Garnish with additional green onion.   *4 servings*

Prep time: 10 minutes
Cooking time: 15 minutes

MICROWAVE: • Reduce margarine to 2 tablespoons. • Microwave red peppers, onions and margarine in 2-quart casserole on HIGH 1 to 2 minutes or until vegetables are crisp-tender. • Stir in potatoes, meat and seasonings; cover with lid. • Microwave 10 to 17 minutes or until potatoes are cooked and mixture is thoroughly heated, stirring every 5 minutes. • Stir in process cheese food; cover. • Microwave 2 minutes or until process cheese food is melted. Garnish with additional green onion.

Microwave cooking time: 21 minutes

SIDE DISHES

CREAMY GREEN BEANS AND MUSHROOMS

(photographed on previous page)

1½ cups mushroom slices
 2 tablespoons PARKAY Margarine
 3 tablespoons dry white wine
 ¼ teaspoon dried thyme leaves,
    crushed

 1 lb. hot cooked green beans
 ¼ lb. VELVEETA Pasteurized Process
    Cheese Spread, cubed

Saute mushrooms in margarine. Stir in wine and thyme; cook 1 minute. Reduce heat to low.

Add beans and process cheese spread; stir until process cheese spread is melted. Garnish with sauteed red pepper strips, mushroom caps and fresh thyme.

4 servings

Prep time: 15 minutes

MICROWAVE: • Reduce margarine to 1 tablespoon and wine to 4½ teaspoons. • Microwave mushrooms and margarine in 2-quart bowl on HIGH 1 to 2 minutes or until mushrooms are tender. • Stir in wine and thyme. Microwave 1 minute. • Stir in beans and process cheese spread. • Microwave 2 to 5 minutes or until process cheese spread is melted. Garnish with sauteed red pepper strips, mushroom caps and fresh thyme.

Microwave cooking time: 8 minutes

Variations: Omit wine. Add 3 tablespoons milk with process cheese spread.

Substitute 16-oz. pkg. frozen cut green beans, cooked, drained, for fresh green beans.

GARLICKY CREAMED SPINACH

 ¼ cup chopped onion
 2 small garlic cloves, minced
 2 tablespoons PARKAY Margarine
 1 (10 oz.) pkg. frozen chopped
    spinach, thawed, drained

 Dash of pepper
 ¼ lb. VELVEETA Pasteurized Process
    Cheese Spread, cubed
 1 tablespoon milk

Saute onions and garlic in margarine. Reduce heat to medium. Stir in spinach and pepper; cook until thoroughly heated. Reduce heat to low.

Add process cheese spread and milk; stir until process cheese spread is melted.

2 to 3 servings

Prep time: 20 minutes

MICROWAVE: • Microwave onions, garlic and margarine in 1-quart bowl on HIGH 1 to 2 minutes or until vegetables are tender. Stir in spinach and pepper.
• Microwave 2 to 3 minutes or until thoroughly heated, stirring after 1½ minutes.
• Add process cheese spread and milk; stir until process cheese spread is melted.

Microwave cooking time: 5 minutes

CHEESY SANTA FE VEGETABLES

1 medium green or red pepper, cut into thin strips
1 medium zucchini, cut into julienne strips
1 medium yellow squash, cut into julienne strips

¼ lb. VELVEETA Mexican Pasteurized Process Cheese Spread with Jalapeño Pepper, cubed
1 tablespoon milk

Place vegetables in 1½-quart bowl. Cover with plastic wrap; vent. Microwave on HIGH 2 to 3 minutes or until crisp-tender, stirring every minute; drain.

Microwave process cheese spread and milk in 1-quart bowl on HIGH 2 to 4 minutes or until process cheese spread is melted, stirring every minute. Serve over vegetables.

4 servings

Prep time: 15 minutes
Microwave cooking time: 7 minutes

CONVENTIONAL: • Steam vegetables over boiling water 2 to 3 minutes or until crisp-tender; drain. • Stir together process cheese spread and milk in saucepan over low heat until process cheese spread is melted. Serve over vegetables.

Conventional cooking time: 10 minutes

CHEESY MASHED POTATO CASSEROLE

½ cup finely chopped leeks
2 garlic cloves, minced
2 tablespoons olive oil
5 cups cooked, cubed, peeled
potatoes (approx. 5 medium)

⅓ cup milk
¼ teaspoon salt
⅛ teaspoon pepper
¼ lb. VELVEETA Pasteurized Process
Cheese Spread, cubed

Preheat oven to 375°.

Saute leeks and garlic in 1 tablespoon oil. Mash potatoes. Add leek mixture, remaining oil, milk and seasonings; beat until fluffy.

Spoon half of potato mixture into 1-quart casserole; cover with process cheese spread and remaining potato mixture.

Bake 25 to 30 minutes or until thoroughly heated. Garnish with additional chopped leeks.
6 to 8 servings

Prep time: 25 minutes
Cooking time: 30 minutes

MICROWAVE: • Microwave leeks, garlic and 1 tablespoon oil in 1-quart casserole on HIGH 1 to 2 minutes or until leeks are tender. Mash potatoes. Add leek mixture, remaining oil, milk and seasonings; beat until fluffy. • Assemble casserole as directed; cover with lid. • Microwave 5 to 8 minutes or until thoroughly heated, turning dish after 3 minutes. Let stand 5 minutes before serving. Garnish with additional leeks.

Microwave cooking time: 10 minutes plus standing

GARDEN RATATOUILLE

½ cup green pepper strips
½ cup red pepper strips
1 small onion, sliced
1 garlic clove, minced
3 tablespoons olive oil
2 cups quartered eggplant slices
  (approx. ¼ inch thick)

1 tomato, chopped
1 teaspoon Italian seasoning
  Dash of black pepper
¼ lb. VELVEETA Pasteurized Process
  Cheese Spread, cubed

Saute pepper strips, onions and garlic in oil. Add eggplant; continue cooking 2 minutes. Reduce heat to low.

Stir in tomatoes and seasonings; cook 1 to 2 minutes or until thoroughly heated. Add process cheese spread; stir until process cheese spread begins to melt.

4 servings

Prep time: 20 minutes

MICROWAVE: • Microwave pepper strips, onions, garlic and oil in 1½-quart bowl on HIGH 2 to 4 minutes or until vegetables are crisp-tender. • Add eggplant. Microwave 2 to 4 minutes or until tender. • Stir in tomatoes and seasonings. Microwave 1 to 2 minutes or until thoroughly heated. Add process cheese spread; stir until process cheese spread begins to melt.

Microwave cooking time: 10 minutes

Left to right: Cheesy Walnut Quick Bread (page 47), Mexican Corn Bread (page 46), Cheesy Scones (page 46), Italian Salami Bread

ITALIAN SALAMI BREAD

1 (16 oz.) pkg. hot roll mix
¾ cup (3 ozs.) VELVEETA Shredded
    Pasteurized Process Cheese
    Food
½ cup chopped OSCAR MAYER Hard
    Salami

¼ cup finely chopped green onion
1 teaspoon Italian seasoning
    Basil Spread

Prepare hot roll mix according to package directions, except omitting margarine. Stir in process cheese food, salami, onions and seasoning.

Knead dough on lightly floured surface 5 minutes or until smooth and elastic. Let rest 5 minutes.

Shape dough into ball; place on greased cookie sheet. Cover; let rise in warm place 30 minutes.

Preheat oven to 375°.

Bake bread 25 to 30 minutes or until golden brown. Serve with Basil Spread.

1 loaf

BASIL SPREAD

½ cup (2 ozs.) VELVEETA Shredded
    Pasteurized Process Cheese
    Food
4 ozs. PHILADELPHIA BRAND Cream
    Cheese, softened

1 tablespoon milk
2 teaspoons chopped fresh basil

Mix together all ingredients until well blended. Garnish with additional fresh basil.

¾ cup

Prep time: 15 minutes plus rising
Cooking time: 30 minutes

CHEESY SCONES

2½ cups buttermilk baking mix
1 cup (4 ozs.) VELVEETA Shredded
    Pasteurized Process Cheese
    Food

⅛ to ¼ teaspoon ground red pepper
⅔ cup milk

Preheat oven to 350°.

Stir together baking mix, process cheese food and pepper.

Add milk; stir until mixture forms dough. If dough is too sticky, gradually stir in up to ¼ cup additional baking mix to make dough easy to handle.

Shape dough into ball; knead on lightly floured surface ten times. Roll out to 10-inch circle. Cut into twelve wedges. Place on greased cookie sheet.

Bake 18 to 20 minutes or until golden brown.

1 dozen

Prep time: 15 minutes
Cooking time: 20 minutes

Variation: Top hot baked scones with additional ½ cup (2 ozs.) VELVEETA Shredded Pasteurized Process Cheese Food. Continue baking until process cheese food begins to melt.

MEXICAN CORN BREAD

¼ lb. VELVEETA Mexican Pasteurized
    Process Cheese Spread with
    Jalapeño Pepper, cubed

2 tablespoons milk
1 egg, beaten
1 (8½ oz.) pkg. corn muffin mix

Preheat oven to 350°.

Stir together process cheese spread and milk in saucepan over low heat until process cheese spread is melted. Add with egg to muffin mix, mixing just until moistened. Pour into greased 8-inch square pan.

Bake 20 minutes.

6 to 8 servings

Prep time: 10 minutes
Cooking time: 20 minutes

Variation: Substitute VELVEETA Pasteurized Process Cheese Spread for VELVEETA Pasteurized Process Cheese Spread with Jalapeño Pepper.

CHEESY WALNUT QUICK BREAD

2½ cups flour
2 tablespoons sugar
1 tablespoon CALUMET Baking Powder
½ teaspoon salt
1 cup (4 ozs.) VELVEETA Shredded Pasteurized Process Cheese Food

¾ cup chopped walnuts
1 cup milk
6 tablespoons PARKAY Margarine, melted
1 egg, beaten

Preheat oven to 350°.

Mix together dry ingredients. Stir in process cheese food and walnuts.

Add combined remaining ingredients, mixing just until moistened. Spoon into greased and floured 9 x 5-inch loaf pan.

Bake 35 to 40 minutes or until wooden pick inserted in center comes out clean. Cool 5 minutes; remove from pan.

1 loaf

Prep time: 10 minutes
Cooking time: 40 minutes

BROCCOLI AND CAULIFLOWER WITH CURRY SAUCE

½ lb. VELVEETA Pasteurized Process Cheese Spread, cubed
2 tablespoons milk
½ teaspoon curry powder
3 cups hot cooked broccoli flowerets, well drained

3 cups hot cooked cauliflowerets, well drained
2 tablespoons chopped unsalted peanuts

Stir together process cheese spread, milk and curry powder in saucepan over low heat until process cheese spread is melted.

Pour over combined vegetables; sprinkle with peanuts.

6 servings

Prep time: 20 minutes

MICROWAVE: • Microwave process cheese spread, milk and curry powder in 1½-quart bowl on HIGH 4 to 6 minutes or until process cheese spread is melted, stirring every 2 minutes. • Continue as directed.

Microwave cooking time: 6 minutes

CREAMY CORN AU GRATIN

½ cup green onion slices
½ cup chopped red pepper
¼ cup PARKAY Margarine
2 (10 oz.) pkgs. frozen whole kernel
   corn, thawed, drained

½ lb. VELVEETA Pasteurized Process
   Cheese Spread, cubed
⅔ cup crushed tortilla chips
½ teaspoon Mexican seasoning
2 tablespoons chopped cilantro

Saute onions and peppers in 2 tablespoons margarine. Reduce heat to low.

Stir in corn and process cheese spread. Cook 5 to 7 minutes or until process cheese spread is melted and mixture is thoroughly heated, stirring occasionally.

Melt remaining margarine in separate pan; stir in tortilla chips and seasoning. Cook over medium heat 3 minutes; stir in cilantro.

Spoon corn mixture into serving bowl; sprinkle with tortilla mixture. Garnish with additional cilantro and red pepper.

6 servings

Prep time: 25 minutes

MICROWAVE: • Microwave onions, peppers and 2 tablespoons margarine in 1½-quart bowl on HIGH 2 to 3 minutes or until vegetables are tender. • Stir in corn and process cheese spread. Microwave 5 to 7 minutes or until process cheese spread is melted and mixture is thoroughly heated, stirring every 3 minutes.
• Microwave remaining margarine in 1-quart bowl 1 minute. Stir in tortilla chips and seasoning. Microwave 2 minutes, stirring after 1 minute; stir in cilantro. • Continue as directed.

Microwave cooking time: 13 minutes

Variation: Substitute ¼ teaspoon ground cumin and ¼ teaspoon chili powder for Mexican seasoning.

Creamy Corn au Gratin

EASY ENTERTAINING

PEA POD 'N GINGER CHICKEN SALAD

(photographed on previous page)

¼ **cup KRAFT Real Mayonnaise**
¼ **cup sour cream**
2 **teaspoons minced peeled ginger root**
½ **teaspoon grated lime peel**
1½ **cups chopped cooked chicken**

½ **cup celery slices**
¼ **lb. Chinese pea pods, blanched, cut in half crosswise**
¼ **lb. VELVEETA Pasteurized Process Cheese Spread, cubed**
Salt and pepper

Mix together mayonnaise, sour cream, ginger root and lime peel. Stir in chicken, celery and pea pods. Chill.

Stir in process cheese spread just before serving. Season with salt and pepper to taste. Serve in Pastry Salad Shell (recipe follows), if desired.   *6 to 8 servings*

Prep time: 15 minutes plus chilling

PASTRY SALAD SHELL

⅔ **cup cold water**
¼ **cup PARKAY Margarine**
1 **cup flour**
1½ **teaspoons dry mustard**
¼ **teaspoon salt**

¼ **teaspoon crushed red pepper**
4 **eggs**
¼ **lb. VELVEETA Pasteurized Process Cheese Spread, cubed**

Preheat oven to 375°.

Bring water and margarine to boil in 2-quart saucepan. Reduce heat to low. Add flour, mustard, salt and red pepper; stir vigorously until mixture forms a ball. Remove from heat.

Spoon into large bowl of electric mixer. Add eggs, one at a time, beating at medium speed of electric mixer after each addition until well blended. Mix in process cheese spread. Spread mixture evenly over bottom and 3 inches up sides of lightly greased 9-inch springform pan.

Bake 35 minutes or until puffed and golden brown. Turn off oven. Prick shell with fork 6 to 8 times. Return to oven for 10 minutes to dry. Remove from oven; cool slightly. Loosen shell from rim of pan; remove from pan. Cool.

Fill with Pea Pod 'n Ginger Chicken Salad (recipe above) or your favorite salad filling, if desired.   *1 shell*

Prep time: 15 minutes
Cooking time: 35 minutes plus drying

MEXICAN-STYLE STEAK WITH PEPPERS

¼ cup oil
3 tablespoons lime juice
3 tablespoons Worcestershire sauce
2 garlic cloves, minced
1 tablespoon finely chopped fresh jalapeño peppers
1 (1½ lb.) beef top round steak, 1 inch thick

½ green pepper, cut into wedges
½ red pepper, cut into wedges
½ yellow pepper, cut into wedges
½ lb. VELVEETA Mexican Pasteurized Process Cheese Spread with Jalapeño Pepper, cubed
2 tablespoons beer or chicken broth

Mix together oil, 2 tablespoons lime juice, Worcestershire sauce, garlic and jalapeño peppers. Pour over steak. Cover; marinate in refrigerator 8 to 12 hours, turning occasionally.

Drain, reserving oil mixture.

Preheat electric broiler or grill (not necessary to preheat gas broiler).

Place steak on rack of broiler pan so top is 2 to 3 inches from heat (or place meat on greased grill over medium coals; coals will be glowing slightly).

Broil (or grill) 7 minutes. Turn steak; surround with pepper wedges.

Continue broiling (or grilling) 7 to 9 minutes or to desired doneness, brushing steak and pepper wedges frequently with reserved oil mixture.

Stir together remaining lime juice, process cheese spread and beer in saucepan over low heat until process cheese spread is melted.

Carve steak across grain into thin slices. Serve with pepper wedges and process cheese spread sauce.

4 to 6 servings

Prep time: 20 minutes plus marinating
Cooking time: 16 minutes

GINGER SHRIMP AND GREEN BEANS

1 lb. cleaned uncooked shrimp
½ lb. green beans, cut into 2-inch pieces
1 tablespoon minced peeled ginger root
2 teaspoons grated lemon peel
1 to 2 red chili peppers, seeded, finely chopped

2 tablespoons PARKAY Margarine
½ lb. VELVEETA Pasteurized Process Cheese Spread, cubed
2 tablespoons milk
6 ozs. angel hair pasta, cooked, drained

Saute shrimp, beans, ginger root, lemon peel and peppers in margarine over medium heat 3 to 5 minutes or until shrimp are pink. Reduce heat to low.

Add process cheese spread and milk; stir until process cheese spread is melted. Serve over hot pasta.   *4 servings*

Prep time: 25 minutes

CREAMY CHICKEN CACCIATORE

1 (2½ to 3 lb.) broiler-fryer, cut up
1 large onion, sliced, separated into rings
2 tablespoons PARKAY Margarine
1 cup chopped tomato
1 cup green pepper strips
½ cup dry white wine or chicken broth

1½ teaspoons dried oregano leaves, crushed
½ teaspoon black pepper
½ lb. VELVEETA Pasteurized Process Cheese Spread, cubed
¼ cup sour cream

Brown chicken with onion in margarine in large skillet. Add tomatoes, green peppers, wine and seasonings.

Bring to boil. Reduce heat to medium-low; cover. Simmer 20 minutes or until chicken is tender. Remove cover. Continue cooking 10 minutes. Reduce heat to low. Remove chicken to platter, reserving drippings in skillet; keep warm.

Add process cheese spread and sour cream to drippings in skillet; stir until process cheese spread is melted. Serve over chicken.   *4 servings*

Prep time: 20 minutes
Cooking time: 30 minutes

Ginger Shrimp and Green Beans

Tomatillo Appetizer Pizza

TOMATILLO APPETIZER PIZZA

½ (15 oz.) pkg. refrigerated pie crust (1 crust)
4 tomatillos, husks removed*
¼ cup chopped onion
1 to 2 fresh jalapeño peppers, halved, seeded
1 garlic clove, halved
1 cup cold water

⅓ cup loosely packed cilantro leaves
¾ cup (6 ozs.) VELVEETA Mexican Shredded Pasteurized Process Cheese Food
¼ cup green pepper strips
¼ cup red pepper strips
2 tablespoons pine nuts, toasted

Preheat oven to 450°.

Unfold pie crust onto greased cookie sheet; prick with fork. Bake 7 to 8 minutes or until lightly browned.

Reduce oven temperature to 350°.

Cook tomatillos, onions, jalapeño peppers and garlic in water 10 minutes or until tomatillos are tender; drain. Place tomatillo mixture and cilantro in blender or food processor container with steel blade attached. Cover; process until smooth.

Spread tomatillo mixture over crust. Top with process cheese food, green and red peppers and pine nuts.

Bake 5 to 7 minutes or until process cheese food is melted. Cut into wedges; serve warm.

10 appetizers

Prep time: 20 minutes
Cooking time: 7 minutes

*Tomatillos are a Mexican variety of green tomatoes and can be purchased in the produce section of your supermarket or in specialty food stores.

LAYERED MEXICAN TACO DINNER

8 cups broken tortilla chips
¾ lb. VELVEETA Mexican Pasteurized
    Process Cheese Spread with
    Jalapeño Pepper, cubed
1 lb. ground beef
1 cup chopped green pepper

1 cup salsa
¼ cup sour cream
½ cup chopped tomato
½ cup thin zucchini slices
2 tablespoons chopped cilantro

Preheat oven to 350°.

Line bottom of 13 x 9-inch baking dish with chips; top with half of process cheese spread.

Brown meat; drain. Add peppers and salsa. Cover; simmer 5 minutes or until peppers are tender. Stir in sour cream; spoon over chips. Top with tomatoes, zucchini and remaining process cheese spread.

Bake 5 minutes or until process cheese spread is melted. Sprinkle with cilantro.

6 to 8 servings

Prep time: 20 minutes
Cooking time: 5 minutes

PORK CHOPS 'N STUFFING BAKE

8 pork loin chops, 1 inch thick
¼ cup PARKAY Margarine
1 cup celery slices
½ cup green onion slices
½ cup chopped red pepper
1 (14½ oz.) can chicken broth with
    reduced salt
¾ cup cold water

½ to 1 teaspoon dried rosemary
    leaves, crushed
1 (16 oz.) pkg. herb seasoned
    stuffing mix
2 cups (8 ozs.) VELVEETA Shredded
    Pasteurized Process Cheese
    Food

Preheat oven to 350°.

Brown chops in 2 tablespoons margarine in large skillet. Remove chops.

Saute celery, onions and peppers in remaining margarine in same skillet. Stir in broth, water and rosemary. Stir in stuffing mix until moistened; stir in process cheese food. Place in greased 13 x 9-inch baking dish. Arrange chops over stuffing; cover.

Bake 40 to 45 minutes or until chops are tender.

8 servings

Prep time: 20 minutes
Cooking time: 45 minutes

MUSHROOM STUFFED CHICKEN BREASTS

**2 boneless skinless chicken breasts
(approx. ¾ lb.)**
1 cup finely chopped mushrooms
**3 tablespoons dry sherry or chicken
broth**

2 tablespoons PARKAY Margarine
**¼ lb. VELVEETA Pasteurized Process
Cheese Spread, cubed**
¾ teaspoon dill weed

Preheat oven to 350°.

Pound chicken to ¼-inch thickness.

Saute mushrooms in 1 tablespoon sherry and 1 tablespoon margarine until moisture evaporates. Stir in ¼ cup process cheese spread and ½ teaspoon dill.

Spoon evenly over chicken breasts. Roll up, starting at narrow end; secure with wooden picks. Place, seam side down, in 10 x 6-inch baking dish. Brush with remaining margarine, melted; cover.

Bake 25 to 30 minutes or until tender. Remove wooden picks.

Stir together remaining sherry, remaining process cheese spread and remaining dill in saucepan over low heat until process cheese spread is melted. Serve over chicken. *2 servings*

Prep time: 20 minutes
Cooking time: 30 minutes

MICROWAVE: • Reduce sherry to 2 teaspoons and margarine to 1 tablespoon. • Pound chicken to ¼-inch thickness. • Stir together mushrooms, 1 teaspoon sherry and 1 tablespoon margarine in 1-quart bowl. Microwave on HIGH 4 to 7 minutes or until moisture evaporates, stirring after 3 minutes. • Pat mushroom mixture dry. Stir in ¼ cup process cheese spread and ½ teaspoon dill. • Spoon mixture evenly over chicken breasts. Roll up as directed. • Place, seam side down, in 9-inch pie plate. Cover with plastic wrap; vent. • Microwave 3 to 4 minutes or until chicken is tender, turning dish after 2 minutes. Let stand, covered, while preparing sauce. • Stir together remaining sherry, remaining process cheese spread and remaining dill in 1-quart bowl. Microwave 30 seconds to 1 minute or until process cheese spread is melted when stirred. Remove wooden picks from chicken; top with sauce.

Microwave cooking time: 12 minutes

TEX-MEX FONDUE

¼ cup tequila or chicken broth
1 garlic clove, minced
1 lb. VELVEETA Mexican Pasteurized
   Process Cheese Spread with
   Jalapeño Pepper, cubed

2 tablespoons lime juice
2 tablespoons chopped cilantro

Heat tequila and garlic in medium saucepan or fondue pot. Bring to boil. Reduce heat to low; simmer 1 minute.

Add process cheese spread and lime juice; stir until process cheese spread is melted. Stir in chopped cilantro. Garnish with cilantro sprig.

Serve hot with jicama chunks, bell pepper chunks and tortilla chips.   *4 servings*

Prep time: 10 minutes

CHEESY STROMBOLI SANDWICH

1 (1 lb.) Italian bread loaf
½ lb. ground beef
1 cup chopped red onion
¼ lb. pepperoni, chopped
1 large tomato, chopped

2 cups chopped fresh spinach
¼ cup pizza sauce
1½ teaspoons Italian seasoning
½ lb. VELVEETA Pasteurized Process
   Cheese Spread, cubed

Preheat oven to 400°.

Cut ½-inch lengthwise slice from top of bread loaf; reserve for later use. Remove center from bread loaf, leaving 1-inch-thick shell.

Brown ground beef; drain. Add onions; cook until tender. Add pepperoni, tomatoes, spinach, pizza sauce and seasoning; cook 3 minutes, stirring occasionally. Reduce heat to low.

Add process cheese spread; stir until process cheese spread begins to melt.

Fill shell with meat mixture; cover with top of bread loaf. Wrap in foil.

Bake 12 to 15 minutes or until thoroughly heated.   *8 servings*

Prep time: 30 minutes
Cooking time: 15 minutes

Tex-Mex Fondue

ASPARAGUS BUNDLES

1 cup mushroom slices
1 cup thin red pepper strips
¾ cup PARKAY Margarine, melted
1½ teaspoons dried summer savory leaves, crushed
¼ to ½ teaspoon black pepper

2 (10 oz.) pkgs. frozen asparagus spears, thawed, well drained
16 frozen phyllo sheets, thawed
2 cups (8 ozs.) VELVEETA Shredded Pasteurized Process Cheese Food

Preheat oven to 375°.

Saute mushrooms and red peppers in 1 tablespoon margarine 3 to 5 minutes or until all moisture evaporates. Stir in savory and black pepper. Remove from heat; set aside.

Divide asparagus into eight equal portions.

Brush one phyllo sheet with margarine. Top with second phyllo sheet; brush with margarine. Place one portion asparagus, ¼ cup process cheese food and 2 tablespoons vegetable mixture on one end of dough. Fold short sides of dough over filling; brush lightly with margarine. Roll lengthwise to form bundle. Repeat with remaining phyllo and filling.

Place bundles on greased cookie sheet; brush tops lightly with margarine.

Bake 18 to 20 minutes or until golden brown.   *8 servings*

Prep time: 30 minutes
Cooking time: 20 minutes

ANTIPASTO PASTA SALAD

1 large red pepper
1 (6½ oz.) jar marinated artichoke hearts, undrained
1 (14 oz.) can hearts of palm, drained, sliced
3 cups (6 ozs.) large bow tie pasta, cooked, drained

1 medium zucchini, sliced
½ cup capocollo ham strips
1 (8 oz.) bottle KRAFT House Italian Dressing
¾ lb. VELVEETA Pasteurized Process Cheese Spread, cubed

Preheat electric broiler (not necessary to preheat gas broiler).

Place whole pepper on rack of broiler pan so top is 4 to 5 inches from heat.

Broil 4 to 5 minutes on each side or until skin of pepper is blistered and brown. Place in paper bag; let stand 5 minutes. Remove skin, stem, seeds and membranes from pepper; cut into strips.

Drain artichokes, reserving marinade. Cut artichoke hearts into smaller pieces, if desired.

Mix together reserved marinade, pepper strips, artichokes and all remaining ingredients except process cheese spread. Chill.

Stir in process cheese spread just before serving.   *8 servings*

Prep time: 25 minutes plus chilling

Variation: Substitute OSCAR MAYER Hard Salami for ham.

CHEESY ARTICHOKE SQUARES

1 **frozen ready-to-bake puff pastry sheet**
3 **eggs**
1 **(6½ oz.) jar marinated artichoke hearts, undrained**
1 **garlic clove, minced**
1 **cup (4 ozs.) VELVEETA Shredded Pasteurized Process Cheese Food**

2 **tablespoons dry bread crumbs**
1 **tablespoon chopped parsley**
½ **teaspoon dried oregano leaves, crushed**
¼ **teaspoon hot pepper sauce**

Preheat oven to 375°.

Thaw pastry sheet according to package directions.

Roll pastry to 12-inch square on lightly floured surface. With sharp knife, cut 11-inch square in center of sheet, leaving 1-inch border all the way around.

Remove center square; place on ungreased cookie sheet. Beat one egg; lightly brush over pastry square.

Cross two opposite corners of 1-inch border over each other and pull through to form 10-inch square. Place on outside edges of center square to form rim. Brush border with remaining beaten egg.

Bake 10 minutes.

Drain marinade from artichoke hearts into small skillet. Chop artichokes; set aside. Saute garlic in marinade.

Mix together remaining two eggs, beaten, artichokes, garlic mixture, process cheese food, bread crumbs, parsley, oregano and hot pepper sauce. Spoon into partially baked pastry shell. Continue baking 20 minutes or until puffed and golden brown. Cut into squares.   *Approximately 1½ dozen*

Prep time: 15 minutes plus thawing
Cooking time: 20 minutes

SANDWICHES & MORE

TASTY CHICKEN TACO SALAD

(photographed on previous page)

1 (1.25 oz.) pkg. taco
    seasoning mix
¾ cup cold water
4 boneless skinless chicken breasts
    (approx. 1¼ lbs.), cooked, cut
    into strips
3 cups tortilla chips
3 cups shredded lettuce

1 cup julienne-cut jicama
1 avocado, peeled, sliced
1 tomato, chopped
¼ lb. VELVEETA Mexican Pasteurized
    Process Cheese Spread with
    Jalapeño Pepper, cubed
    Chopped cilantro

Mix together seasoning mix and water in saucepan. Simmer 5 minutes or until slightly thickened. Stir in chicken.

Arrange chips in serving dish. Top with chicken mixture, lettuce, jicama, avocados, tomatoes and process cheese spread. Sprinkle with cilantro. Serve with sour cream and garnish with cilantro sprig. *4 to 6 servings*

Prep time: 40 minutes

SPECIAL STUFFED HAMBURGERS

1½ lbs. ground beef
1 tablespoon Dijon mustard
1 teaspoon dill weed
¼ lb. VELVEETA Pasteurized Process
    Cheese Spread, cut into four
    slices

1 medium onion, sliced
1 tablespoon PARKAY Margarine
4 Kaiser rolls or hamburger buns,
    split, toasted
    KRAFT Thousand Island Dressing

Preheat electric broiler (not necessary to preheat gas broiler).

Mix together meat, mustard and dill; shape into eight 5-inch patties.

Place one process cheese spread slice on each of four patties; top with remaining patties. Pinch edges of patties together to seal.

Place patties on rack of broiler pan so tops are 3 to 4 inches from heat. Broil 5 to 7 minutes on each side or to desired doneness.

Saute onions in margarine. Fill rolls with patties; top with onions and dressing.

4 sandwiches

Prep time: 15 minutes
Cooking time: 14 minutes

MEXICAN SUBMARINE SANDWICHES

1 lb. chorizo sausage*
4 bolillos (Mexican-style rolls) or
   French bread rolls, split, toasted
   Sour cream
1 cup shredded lettuce

½ lb. VELVEETA Mexican Pasteurized
   Process Cheese Spread with
   Jalapeño Pepper, sliced
1 avocado, peeled, sliced
1 tomato, sliced

Remove sausage from casing. Brown sausage; drain.

Spread rolls with sour cream; fill with sausage and remaining ingredients.

4 sandwiches

Prep time: 15 minutes

*Chorizo sausage is a Mexican variety of sausage and can be purchased in specialty food stores.

MARINATED STEAK PASTA SALAD

¼ cup oil
3 tablespoons lime juice
1 tablespoon chopped fresh
   jalapeño peppers
2 garlic cloves, minced
½ lb. beef flank steak
3 cups (8 ozs.) radiatore pasta or
   rotini, cooked, drained

½ cup green pepper strips
½ small red onion, cut into thin
   wedges
½ lb. VELVEETA Mexican Pasteurized
   Process Cheese Spread with
   Jalapeño Pepper, cubed

Mix together oil, lime juice, jalapeño peppers and garlic; pour over steak. Cover; marinate in refrigerator 1 hour. Drain, reserving oil mixture.

Preheat electric broiler (not necessary to preheat gas broiler).

Place steak on rack of broiler pan so top is 2 to 3 inches from heat.

Broil 4 to 5 minutes on each side or to desired doneness.

Carve steak across grain into thin slices; halve crosswise. Toss steak slices with pasta, green peppers and onions.

Bring reserved oil mixture to boil. Reduce heat to low. Add process cheese spread; stir until melted. Pour over pasta mixture; serve immediately. *4 to 6 servings*

Prep time: 15 minutes plus marinating
Cooking time: 10 minutes

CHEESY PANCAKES WITH APPLE CINNAMON TOPPING

2 cups buttermilk baking mix
1½ cups (6 ozs.) VELVEETA Shredded
    Pasteurized Process Cheese
    Food
1 cup milk
2 eggs

¼ teaspoon grated lemon peel
2 medium apples, sliced
2 tablespoons PARKAY Margarine
¼ cup packed brown sugar
½ teaspoon ground cinnamon

Preheat electric griddle to 350°.

Beat baking mix, process cheese food, milk, eggs and lemon peel. For each of twelve pancakes, pour approximately ¼ cup batter onto hot greased griddle.

Cook until edges are dry. Turn; cook until golden. Remove from griddle; keep warm.

Saute apples in margarine in skillet until tender. Stir in sugar and cinnamon; heat thoroughly. Serve over pancakes.

4 servings

Prep time: 15 minutes

GRILLED FRENCH TOAST WITH NUTTY FILLING

¼ lb. VELVEETA Pasteurized Process
    Cheese Spread, cubed
¼ cup PHILADELPHIA BRAND Soft
    Cream Cheese
⅓ cup sliced almonds, toasted
⅓ cup raisins

4 (1¼ inch thick) white bread slices
3 eggs, beaten
⅓ cup milk
½ teaspoon grated orange peel
2 tablespoons PARKAY Margarine
    Powdered sugar

Beat process cheese spread and cream cheese at medium speed with electric mixer until well blended. Stir in almonds and raisins.

Cut slit through top crust of each bread slice almost to bottom crust to form pocket. Fill each pocket with ¼ cup process cheese spread mixture; press slightly to close.

Preheat electric griddle to 350°.

Dip each bread slice into combined eggs, milk and orange peel in shallow dish. Grill on both sides in margarine until golden brown. Sprinkle with powdered sugar.

4 servings

Prep time: 30 minutes

Cheesy Pancakes with Apple Cinnamon Topping

Hearty Breakfast Rolls

HEARTY BREAKFAST ROLLS

1 (8 oz.) pkg. refrigerated crescent dinner rolls
2 tablespoons KRAFT Strawberry or Apricot Preserves
6 OSCAR MAYER Smoked Cooked Ham Slices

¾ cup (3 ozs.) VELVEETA Shredded Pasteurized Process Cheese Food

Preheat oven to 350°.

Unroll dough into two rectangles; firmly press perforations together to seal. Spread rectangles with preserves; top with ham and process cheese food.

Roll up each rectangle, starting at narrow end; seal edge. Cut each roll into four slices. Place, cut side down, in greased 8-inch pie plate or round cake pan.

Bake 25 to 30 minutes or until golden brown

8 servings

Prep time: 15 minutes
Cooking time: 30 minutes

BEEF BARLEY SOUP

½ lb. ground beef
2½ cups cold water
1 (14½ oz.) can stewed tomatoes, cut up
¾ cup carrot slices
¾ cup mushroom slices
½ cup quick barley, uncooked

2 garlic cloves, minced
1 teaspoon dried oregano leaves, crushed
½ lb. VELVEETA Pasteurized Process Cheese Spread, cubed
Salt and pepper

Brown meat in large saucepan; drain. Stir in water, tomatoes, carrots, mushrooms, barley, garlic and oregano.

Bring to boil. Reduce heat to low; cover. Simmer 10 minutes or until barley is tender.

Add process cheese spread; stir until melted. Season with salt and pepper to taste.

Six 1-cup servings

Prep time: 35 minutes

Thai Chicken Salad

THAI CHICKEN SALAD

3 tablespoons creamy peanut
    butter
3 tablespoons sugar
1 teaspoon crushed red pepper
⅔ cup KRAFT "Zesty" Italian Dressing
1 tablespoon soy sauce

2 boneless skinless chicken breasts
    (approx. ¾ lb.), cooked, cut
    into thin strips
¼ lb. VELVEETA Pasteurized Process
    Cheese Spread, cubed
½ cup julienne-cut carrots
½ cup red or green pepper strips
¼ cup chopped roasted peanuts

Mix together peanut butter, sugar and red pepper. Stir in dressing and soy sauce.

Toss together ½ cup dressing mixture with combined remaining ingredients. Serve with remaining dressing mixture.

4 servings

Prep time: 30 minutes

SPICY SOUTHWEST CORN SOUP

1 (10 oz.) pkg. frozen whole kernel
    corn, thawed, drained
1 garlic clove, minced
1 tablespoon PARKAY Margarine
1 cup chicken broth

1 cup milk
½ lb. VELVEETA Mexican Pasteurized
    Process Cheese Spread with
    Jalapeño Pepper, cubed
2 tablespoons chopped cilantro

Saute corn and garlic in margarine in large saucepan. Reduce heat to low.

Add remaining ingredients; stir until process cheese spread is melted and soup is thoroughly heated. Top individual servings with crushed tortilla chips, if desired.

Four 1-cup servings

Prep time: 15 minutes

MICROWAVE: • Reduce chicken broth to ¾ cup. • Mix together corn, garlic and margarine in 2-quart casserole; cover with lid. Microwave on HIGH 2 to 3 minutes or until garlic is tender and corn is hot, stirring every minute. • Stir in remaining ingredients. Microwave 5 to 7 minutes or until process cheese spread is melted and soup is thoroughly heated, stirring after 4 minutes. • Serve as directed.

Microwave cooking time: 10 minutes

CHEESY SAUSAGE STRATA

½ lb. bulk pork sausage
¾ cup mushroom slices
¼ cup green onion slices
½ lb. VELVEETA Pasteurized Process
    Cheese Spread, cubed

4 cups (¾ inch) crustless sourdough
    bread cubes
1 cup milk
4 eggs, beaten

Brown sausage; drain. Add vegetables. Continue cooking 5 minutes; drain. Let cool 10 minutes.

Stir in process cheese spread and bread cubes; spoon into greased 8-inch square baking dish.

Beat milk and eggs. Pour over sausage mixture; cover. Refrigerate several hours or overnight.

Preheat oven to 350°.

Remove cover. Bake 50 to 55 minutes or until golden brown. Let stand 10 minutes before serving. Garnish with fresh rosemary. *6 servings*

Prep time: 20 minutes plus chilling
Cooking time: 55 minutes plus standing

TASTY TORTILLA SCRAMBLED EGGS

1 medium zucchini, shredded
1 cup broken tortilla chips
1 garlic clove, minced
3 tablespoons PARKAY Margarine

6 eggs, beaten
½ lb. VELVEETA Mexican Pasteurized
    Process Cheese Spread, cubed

Pat zucchini dry on paper towels.

Saute zucchini, chips and garlic in margarine in nonstick skillet 3 to 5 minutes or until chips begin to brown. Reduce heat to low.

Add eggs; cook slowly, stirring occasionally, until eggs begin to set.

Add process cheese spread; continue cooking, stirring occasionally, until process cheese spread is melted and eggs are set. Serve with salsa. *4 servings*

Prep time: 20 minutes

Cheesy Sausage Strata

MUSHROOM QUICHE WITH BROWN RICE CRUST

2½ cups cooked brown rice
3 eggs
1 teaspoon chopped fresh
   rosemary
2 cups (8 ozs.) VELVEETA Shredded
   Pasteurized Process Cheese
   Food

1 cup chopped cooked chicken
1 cup mushroom slices
¾ cup milk
⅛ teaspoon pepper

Preheat oven to 350°.

Mix together rice, one egg, beaten, and ½ teaspoon rosemary. Press onto bottom and up sides of lightly greased 9-inch quiche dish or pie plate to form crust.

Bake 10 minutes.

Mix together remaining two eggs, beaten, remaining rosemary and all other remaining ingredients. Pour into crust.

Bake 50 to 55 minutes or until filling is set. Garnish as desired.   *8 servings*

Prep time: 20 minutes
Cooking time: 55 minutes

WARM CHICKEN SALAD WITH LEMON-DILL DRESSING

4 boneless skinless chicken breasts
   (approx. 1¼ lbs.)
1 tablespoon oil
1 avocado, peeled, sliced
1 tomato, cut into wedges
   Pitted ripe olives

Lettuce
¼ lb. VELVEETA Pasteurized Process
   Cheese Spread, cubed
⅓ cup sour cream
½ teaspoon grated lemon peel
¼ teaspoon dill weed

Cook chicken in oil over medium heat 3 to 5 minutes on each side or until tender; cut into ¼-inch slices.

Arrange chicken, avocados, tomatoes and olives on individual lettuce-covered plates.

Stir together remaining ingredients in saucepan over low heat until process cheese spread is melted; pour over salad.   *4 servings*

Prep time: 30 minutes

Mushroom Quiche with Brown Rice Crust

CHEESY STEAK SANDWICH

1 large onion, cut into thin wedges
1 medium green pepper, cut into
   strips
1 garlic clove, minced
2 tablespoons PARKAY Margarine
¾ lb. rare cooked roast beef slices,
   cut into ½-inch strips

½ lb. VELVEETA Pasteurized Process
   Cheese Spread, cubed
¼ teaspoon black pepper
4 French bread rolls, split, toasted

Saute onions, green peppers and garlic in margarine in large skillet. Reduce heat to low.

Add meat, process cheese spread and black pepper; stir until process cheese spread is melted and meat is thoroughly heated. Fill rolls with meat mixture.

4 sandwiches

Prep time: 25 minutes

MICROWAVE: • Mix together onions, green peppers, garlic and margarine in 2-quart casserole; cover with lid. Microwave on HIGH 5 to 7 minutes or until vegetables are tender, stirring after 4 minutes. • Add meat, process cheese spread and black pepper. Microwave 3 to 4 minutes or until process cheese spread is melted and meat is thoroughly heated, stirring after 2 minutes. • Serve as directed.

Microwave cooking time: 11 minutes

EASY THREE BEAN SALAD

1 (8 oz.) bottle KRAFT House Italian
   Dressing
1 tablespoon Dijon mustard
1 (15 oz.) can kidney beans,
   drained
1 (15 oz.) can garbanzo beans,
   drained

1 (9 oz.) pkg. frozen cut green
   beans, thawed, drained
½ small red onion, cut into thin
   wedges
¼ lb. VELVEETA Pasteurized Process
   Cheese Spread, cubed

Mix together dressing and mustard in large bowl. Stir in beans and onions. Chill.

Stir in process cheese spread just before serving.

6 servings

Prep time: 10 minutes plus chilling

UPSIDE-DOWN PIZZA POT PIE

1 lb. Italian sausage
½ cup chopped onion
½ cup green pepper chunks
½ cup yellow pepper chunks
½ lb. VELVEETA Pasteurized Process
    Cheese Spread, cubed

1 large tomato, chopped
1 teaspoon Italian seasoning
1 (10 oz.) pkg. refrigerated pizza
    crust

Preheat oven to 350°.

Remove sausage from casing. Cook sausage, onions and peppers over medium-high heat 10 to 12 minutes or until sausage is browned and vegetables are tender; drain. Remove from heat.

Stir in process cheese spread, tomatoes and seasoning. Spoon into four (12 ounce) baking dishes.

Unroll pizza dough; cut into four rectangles. Place over sausage mixture; press dough to edge of dish to seal.

Bake 18 to 20 minutes or until golden brown.

4 servings

Prep time: 20 minutes
Cooking time: 20 minutes

GREAT GRILLED TURKEY SANDWICHES

8 whole-wheat bread slices
¼ cup PHILADELPHIA BRAND Soft
    Cream Cheese with Pineapple
4 VELVEETA Pasteurized Process
    Cheese Spread Slices

Spinach leaves
4 OSCAR MAYER Oven Roasted
    Boneless Turkey Breast Slices
Soft PARKAY Margarine

For each sandwich, spread one bread slice with 1 tablespoon cream cheese. Cover with one process cheese spread slice, spinach, turkey and second bread slice.

Spread sandwich with margarine. Grill until lightly browned on both sides.

4 sandwiches

Prep time: 15 minutes

Hot Pita Pockets

HOT PITA POCKETS

¼ lb. VELVEETA Pasteurized Process
    Cheese Spread, cubed
¼ lb. roast beef slices
½ cup broccoli flowerets
¼ cup bean sprouts
¼ cup shredded carrot

1 tablespoon green onion slices
2 whole-wheat pita bread rounds,
    cut in half
8 tomato slices
½ cup plain yogurt
2 teaspoons spicy brown mustard

Toss together process cheese spread, meat, broccoli, bean sprouts, carrots and onions. Fill each pita bread half with two tomato slices and ½ cup process cheese spread mixture.

Microwave on HIGH 3 to 5 minutes or until process cheese spread begins to melt, turning after 2 minutes. Serve with combined yogurt and mustard.

4 sandwiches

Prep time: 15 minutes
Microwave cooking time: 5 minutes

CONVENTIONAL: • Preheat oven to 350°. • Assemble sandwiches as directed. • Wrap each sandwich in foil. • Bake 15 minutes or until process cheese spread begins to melt. • Serve as directed.

Conventional cooking time: 15 minutes

CREAMY HAM POTATO SALAD

½ lb. VELVEETA Pasteurized Process
    Cheese Spread, cubed
¾ cup sour cream
1 tablespoon Dijon mustard
½ teaspoon celery seed

4 cups cooked quartered new
    potatoes
1½ cups ham cubes
¼ cup green onion slices

Stir together process cheese spread, sour cream, mustard and celery seed in saucepan over low heat until process cheese spread is melted.

Pour over combined remaining ingredients; mix lightly. Chill.

6 servings

Prep time: 30 minutes plus chilling

SEAFOOD BISQUE

2 leeks, cut in half lengthwise
2 tablespoons PARKAY margarine
3 cups milk
2 cups chopped peeled potatoes
1 (8 oz.) pkg. imitation crab flakes,
    rinsed

½ teaspoon dried thyme leaves,
    crushed
⅛ to ¼ teaspoon hot pepper sauce
½ lb. VELVEETA Pasteurized Process
    Cheese Spread, cubed
2 tablespoons dry sherry (optional)

Thinly slice white portion and 1 inch of light green portion of leeks; saute in margarine.

Add all remaining ingredients except process cheese spread and sherry.

Bring to boil. Reduce heat to low; cover. Simmer 15 minutes or until potatoes are tender.

Add process cheese spread and sherry; stir until process cheese spread is melted. Garnish with fresh chives and lemon peel.   *Approximately six 1-cup servings*

Prep time: 40 minutes

MICROWAVE: • Reduce milk to 2½ cups. • Mix together leeks, margarine and potatoes in 2-quart casserole; cover with lid. Microwave on HIGH 8 to 10 minutes or until vegetables are almost tender. • Stir in milk and all remaining ingredients except process cheese spread and sherry; cover. Microwave 8 to 14 minutes or until potatoes are tender, stirring every 4 minutes. • Add process cheese spread and sherry; stir until process cheese spread is melted. Garnish as directed.

Microwave cooking time: 24 minutes

KID'S COOKING

RACE CAR DINNER

(photographed on previous page)

2 medium zucchini
   (approx. ½ lb. each)
½ lb. ground beef
¼ lb. VELVEETA Pasteurized Process
   Cheese Spread, cubed
1 cup whole kernel corn

¼ cup catsup
   VELVEETA Pasteurized Process
   Cheese Spread (approx. ¾ lb.),
   thickly sliced
4 pretzel sticks

Preheat oven to 350°.

Trim stem ends of zucchini; cut in half lengthwise. Boil 10 minutes or until tender; drain. Scoop out centers, leaving ¼-inch-thick shell.

Brown meat; drain. Reduce heat to low.

Add process cheese spread cubes, corn and catsup; stir until process cheese spread is melted. Spoon into shells; place in shallow baking pan.

Bake 15 minutes or until thoroughly heated.

Cut twenty circles from process cheese spread slices. For each race car, place one zucchini half on serving plate. Position four process cheese spread circles next to each zucchini as wheels. Insert one pretzel into each of four remaining process cheese spread circles; position in each zucchini as steering wheel.   *4 servings*

Prep time: 20 minutes
Cooking time: 15 minutes

MICROWAVE: • Trim stem ends of zucchini; cut in half lengthwise. Place, cut side down, in 8-inch square baking dish. • Microwave on HIGH 4 to 6 minutes or until tender, rearranging after 3 minutes. • Scoop out centers, leaving ¼-inch-thick shell. Return, cut side up, to same baking dish. • Crumble meat into 1½-quart bowl. Microwave 2 to 3 minutes or until meat loses pink color when stirred; drain. • Stir in process cheese spread cubes, corn and catsup. • Microwave 2 to 4 minutes or until process cheese spread is melted, stirring after 1½ minutes. Spoon into shells. • Microwave 1 to 3 minutes or until thoroughly heated. • Assemble as directed.

Microwave cooking time: 16 minutes

FAVORITE FUDGE

1 lb. VELVEETA Pasteurized Process Cheese Spread, cubed
1 lb. PARKAY Margarine, cut into chunks

12 (1 oz.) squares BAKER'S Semi-Sweet Chocolate, halved
1 (2 lb.) bag powdered sugar, sifted
2 teaspoons vanilla

Line 13 x 9-inch baking pan with foil; grease foil.

Stir together process cheese spread and margarine in 2-quart saucepan over medium heat until melted. Add chocolate; stir until melted.

Pour into large bowl of electric mixer.

Add sugar and vanilla. Beat at medium speed with electric mixer until well blended. Pour into prepared pan.

Chill 2 to 3 hours or until set. Cut into squares.   *4½ pounds*

Prep time: 20 minutes plus chilling

Variation: Add 1 cup chopped nuts with sugar.

BREAKFAST TACOS

1 tablespoon PARKAY Margarine
6 eggs, beaten
2 tablespoons milk
1 cup (4 ozs.) VELVEETA Mexican Shredded Pasteurized Process Cheese Food

6 taco shells, heated
½ cup shredded lettuce
½ cup chopped tomato

Melt margarine in skillet over low heat. Add combined eggs and milk.

Cook slowly, stirring occasionally, until eggs are almost set. Stir in ½ cup process cheese food; continue cooking until eggs are set.

Fill taco shells with eggs and remaining ingredients.   *3 servings*

Prep time: 15 minutes

MICROWAVE: • Microwave margarine in 1½-quart casserole on HIGH 30 seconds or until melted. • Add combined eggs and milk; cover with lid. • Microwave 3½ to 4 minutes or until eggs are almost set, stirring after 2 minutes. • Stir in ½ cup process cheese food. • Serve as directed.

Microwave cooking time: 5 minutes

Cheesy Swirled Oatmeal

CHEESY SWIRLED OATMEAL

Old fashioned or quick oats,
   uncooked
Chopped apple
Sugar

Ground cinnamon
VELVEETA Pasteurized Process
   Cheese Spread, cubed

Cook oats according to label directions, except omitting salt and adding 2 tablespoons apple, 1 tablespoon sugar and 1/8 teaspoon cinnamon per serving.

Spoon into serving bowl(s). Place several process cheese spread cubes on top of oatmeal. Let stand 2 minutes. Swirl process cheese spread into oatmeal. Garnish with sliced apple.

Prep time: 15 minutes

KID'S FAVORITE TUNA CASSEROLE

¾ lb. VELVEETA Pasteurized Process
   Cheese Spread, cubed
⅔ cup milk
1 (3 oz.) pkg. PHILADELPHIA BRAND
   Cream Cheese, cubed
3 cups (6 ozs.) medium noodles,
   cooked, drained

1 (10 oz.) pkg. frozen peas, thawed,
   drained
1 (6½ oz.) can tuna, drained, flaked
1 cup crushed potato chips

Preheat oven to 350°.

Stir together process cheese spread, milk and cream cheese in saucepan over low heat until process cheese spread is melted.

Stir in noodles, peas and tuna. Spoon into 2-quart casserole. Top with chips.

Bake 20 to 25 minutes or until thoroughly heated.   *4 to 6 servings*

Prep time: 15 minutes
Cooking time: 25 minutes

MICROWAVE: • Reduce milk to 3 tablespoons. • Microwave process cheese spread, milk and cream cheese in 2-quart casserole on HIGH 3 to 4 minutes or until process cheese spread is melted, stirring after 2 minutes. • Stir in noodles, peas and tuna. • Microwave 3 to 4 minutes or until thoroughly heated, stirring after 2 minutes. • Top with chips.

Microwave cooking time: 8 minutes

BAKED POTATO SAILBOATS

4 medium baking potatoes, baked
¼ cup milk
¼ lb. VELVEETA Pasteurized Process
   Cheese Spread, cubed

4 slices VELVEETA Pasteurized
   Process Cheese Spread
8 pretzel sticks

Preheat oven to 350°.

Cut thin lengthwise slice from top of each potato. Scoop out centers, leaving ⅛-inch-thick shell.

Mash potatoes with milk. Stir in process cheese spread cubes. Spoon into shells.

Bake 8 to 10 minutes or until potatoes are hot and process cheese spread begins to melt.

Cut process cheese spread slices in half diagonally. Thread onto pretzels; insert two pretzels into each potato to resemble sail. *4 servings*

Prep time: 10 minutes plus baking potatoes
Cooking time: 10 minutes

Micowave Tip: • To heat stuffed potatoes, place in shallow baking dish.
• Microwave on HIGH 2 to 3 minutes or until process cheese spread begins to melt.
• Continue as directed.

FAVORITE MAC 'N CHEESE

¼ cup chopped green pepper
¼ cup chopped red pepper
¼ cup chopped onion
2 tablespoons PARKAY Margarine
1 lb. VELVEETA Pasteurized Process
   Cheese Spread, cubed

½ cup milk
2 cups (7 ozs.) elbow macaroni,
   cooked, drained

Preheat oven to 350°.

Saute vegetables in margarine. Reduce heat to low.

Add process cheese spread and milk; stir until process cheese spread is melted. Stir in macaroni; spoon into 2-quart casserole.

Bake 15 minutes. Sprinkle with KRAFT 100% Grated Parmesan Cheese, if desired.

6 servings

Prep time: 15 minutes
Cooking time: 15 minutes

MICROWAVE: • Microwave vegetables and margarine in 2-quart casserole on HIGH 2 to 2½ minutes or until vegetables are crisp-tender. • Add process cheese spread and milk; microwave 3 to 4 minutes or until process cheese spread is melted, stirring after 2 minutes. • Stir in macaroni. Microwave 4 to 6 minutes or until thoroughly heated, stirring after 3 minutes. Sprinkle with KRAFT 100% Grated Parmesan Cheese, if desired.

Microwave cooking time: 13 minutes

DINNER DIPPERS

4 white bread slices, crusts trimmed	½ cup milk
1 tablespoon PARKAY Margarine, melted	2 cups frozen French fried potatoes, cooked
¼ lb. VELVEETA Pasteurized Process Cheese Spread, cubed	4 OSCAR MAYER Wieners, quartered, heated
½ cup Italian-style tomato sauce	2 cups broccoli flowerets

Preheat oven to 400°.

Flatten bread with rolling pin. Fit bread into medium-size muffin pan. Brush with margarine. Bake 8 to 10 minutes or until golden brown. Remove from pan.

Stir together process cheese spread, tomato sauce and milk in saucepan until process cheese spread is melted.

Place bread cup in center of each plate; fill with sauce. Surround with remaining ingredients as dippers.

4 servings

Prep time: 15 minutes

Microwave Tip: To prepare sauce, microwave process cheese spread, tomato sauce and milk in 2-cup bowl on HIGH 2½ to 3 minutes or until process cheese spread is melted, stirring after each minute.

Variations: Omit bread and margarine. Serve sauce in small bowl.

Substitute LOUIS RICH Turkey Franks for wieners.

INDEX

INDEX

INDEX